Selective Ironies

Stephen Alomes

Selective Ironies

'The drink you have when you're not having a drink'
Clayton's drink advertisement 1970s featuring actor
Jack Thompson

Selective Ironies
ISBN 978 1 76109 000 4
Copyright © text and internal illustrations Stephen Alomes 2020
Front cover: *Wattle Lives* (Stephen Alomes, acrylic)
Back cover: *Faces of Trump* (Stephen Alomes, acrylic)

First published 2020 by
GINNINDERRA PRESS
PO Box 3461 Port Adelaide 5015
www.ginninderrapress.com.au

Contents

Foreword ... 7
Preface ... 9

Nature's Journeys
Still Life Mort Wattle Lives ... 13
Innocents Abroad ... 14
Confessions of a Littoralist ... 15
Les peintres anglais ... 17
Michelin Yum Cha Sophisticate ... 18

Politics and Personalities
Faces of the Donald ... 23
Barracking for Obama ... 24
Malcolm Says ... 27
Laura Norder is back ... 29

Twits, Hipsters and Digits
Self-love in the Twitsphere ... 33
Digital Travels Too…Captive of the Screen ... 34
Toxic Twits – (Hazmat Warning!) ... 37
Gone…I was completely GONE! ... 38
Hipsterville ... 39

Summer's Madnesses
Afternoon Sydney Summer ... 43
All Quiet on the Summer Front ... 44

Everyday Life…sort of
Life's a supermarket, c'est la vie ... 47
'Can I carry Sir's books' ... 48
'Retirement' matters ... 49
I left my brain on Ascot Vale Road ... 51

Hapstranging	52
A Class Society – Cattle Class	53
A Class Society – Bourgeois Class	54
Issues need 'tissues'	55

Life and other catastrophes

Paper Blows Hurt	59
Bullies and the Red Cell	61
Formophobia	62
'Executively developed'…almost	63
'Swanning' by the Impatient	64
Grey Skies Blackening – Coronavirus 2020	65
Mal and Genki Our Family	67
Life's Companion?	68
Significance rolls… Significant rolls	70

Naked Truths at Home and Away

Waiting for Evelyn… My Own Census Collector Lady	73
Moi…perdu?… The naked.truth.gov.au	74

Postludes

Footy's changed	77
Definitely Not a Poet – Clayton's Postlude…	79
Definitely Not a Poet, Maate!	80

Foreword

Stephen Alomes is talented and versatile. His many books have covered an array of themes across politics, history, creative arts, sport, and now, through *Selective Ironies*, he has added another feather to his literary cap. He has a way of sharing his wisdom that entertains, whether he is opening our eyes to home truths about our beloved country (*A Nation At Last?*), paying homage to the great game so many of us cherish (*Australian Football: The People's Game 1958–2058*), or giving us valuable insights into popular culture, our ever-changing society, and even France and Japan, in numerous publications.

Inimitably witty, ironic and thought-provoking, his latest offering, *Selective Ironies*, shows yet another side to his personality – contrary to the Clayton's reference, that of a master of contemporary prose poetry.

Libor Mikeska

Libor Mikeska is an Australian/Czech novelist in Germany, author of *Allegro agitato or Neurotically yours* and *Life's a Game You Play* (SilverWood, Bristol, 2012, 2017). He writes music and teaches English at the University of Heidelberg.

Preface

I have always sought to understand contemporary society, its tensions and frustrations and its social characteristics and contradictions.

As a contemporary cultural historian (others have asked 'are you a pop sociologist?'), I have previously explored contemporary Australia and our global world in writing, in several books and in articles on people's experience of sport, nation, politics, expatriation, intellectuals and popular culture.

Then I discovered expressionist portrait painting as a new vehicle to investigate the horrors of contemporary populism, from Pauline Hanson and Tony Abbott to 'the Donald' (Trump), and in Europe, Silvio Berlusconi and Geert Wilders and the authoritarian populists Vladimir Putin and Recep Tayip Erdogan. Painting also offered a window onto the strange AFL world of the Essendon peptides performance drug saga and its principals – James Hird, Andrew Demetriou and the 'peptides' man, Stephen Dank.

In poetry, we come closer to our own experiences and frustrations. *Selective Ironies* explores the little and the dark ironies of everyday life and their consolations, in words and images, in prose poems, supported by my expressionist acrylic paintings and rubber cuts.

Perhaps irony is the Australian condition after centuries of colonial contradictions and the struggle with a difficult land. Or a modern condition in our changing world? Or is it a response to the absurdities in the institutions of our everyday work and life? Or, simply, my own philosophical tendency?

The poems range across diverse subjects: tissues and issues, warming family cats, the less warm toys of mobile phones, commuting, travel, wattle and water, hospitals, forms and paper wars, hipsters and Twitterers, sport, naked truths and poet figures, and people, love and loss.

I believe that the lightness and darkness, and the humour, of these selective ironies have something valuable to say about the interesting times in which we live.

While a few poetry purists are uncomfortable with the 'Clayton's literary tradition' of prose poetry, I enjoy the ways in which it can capture our lives, often through ironic description. Here, it is also complemented by other poems closer to the more personal Wordsworth tradition of 'emotion recollected in tranquillity'.

May I also thank those who have stimulated and guided me: in art, Patricia Goldby, Graeme Drendel and Lazar Krum, and my colleagues; and in writing, Liz Gallois, Dianne Friend, Marcia van Rolfs, Binh Pham and Kate Jones.

Stephen Alomes

Nature's Journeys

Still Life Mort Wattle Lives

Nature morte is not my cup of tea
Seems like old, cold tea
'Still life'
Too still, too dead, too formal
But there's something about wattle
Mimosa
Wattle lives
Bright yellow and green
A riot of colour to see
Shining wildly over the table top
Like another sun
More vital than mere pots
The colour of fun
Brighter than
Mere vases with pretty *fleurs*
Politely confined within
Flowers which now seem dimmed
Wattle lives, *nature morte* fades

Innocents Abroad

Definitely not a Bazza...
Living in an Earls Court of beer and chunder...
More the suburbs for us
From South Hobart
To deepest, or is it far-flung, Muswell Hill
A slow hour on the 134 bus to Charing Cross Road
Made no faster by the sounds of T-Rex
And 'Rocket Man' on Radio One.
We came by boat
Last of a generation
I travelled with a footy
She met a Horse Guard
In a pub
I worked in an office
20 quid plus luncheon vouchers
'Another colonial' was the welcome
A day too late I responded with
'I find England rather quaint'
She faced the Durex problem
Not just 'pass the sticky tape'
The ginger red working class guardsman's
Old white Merc sports car
Was often in the workshop
Not what it seemed
He had also got around
Other wives or partners perhaps
Our parents visited, one by one,
A robbery when my father was there
'An inside job' suggested the coppers,
The guard was a gambler too.

Confessions of a Littoralist

We are a littoral people
entranced by rainbows, by light on water
by waves and sand, despite the flies.
The coast, not the bush, calls me
despite the smell of gums and the yellow of winter wattle.
I leave the literalism to the bush dwellers
who know that life is nasty, brutish and short,
with fire and flood, drought and unbearable heat.
We Australians are littoralists,
people of the coast, the shoreline,
the space between hills and water.
Hills, not mountains, please note.
And those wild soldiers, brave or foolhardy,
are not mountain men but just wild colonial boys.
Not that all littoralists are in harmony.
A big divide exists – between the majority, people like me,
and the minority.
We drive to the esplanade, walk along the beach and rocks,
in summer our feet briefly touch the froth
as the surf becomes at the beach.
But this swimming, surfing and sailing stuff does not appeal.
A few charge in, embracing the waves,
immersing themselves in nature's elements.
Others, more philosophically bent,
look to Jung or feminist environmentalism.
Is their sea part of a collective unconscious?
I glimpse the waves through a car window
while enjoying an ice cream.

More radically, the water is touched lightly,
by slightly sandy, accidentally salty, feet
We need the shores of our dreaming,
but dreaming does not demand diving in
Or even getting wet.

Les peintres anglais

Settled for a week
in a Sicilian villa
avec les peintres anglais
marooned perhaps
in an Agatha Christie country house.
The aquarelle flows
pretty pictures of nature,
pots and ruins.
Charming, proficient, but…
The conversation flows too
like an English stream
bubbling without depth
'Who did it?' I wondered.
Nice people bar one 'grand dame'
who confuses hauteur and arrogance
with civilisation.
Was she embarrassed when
the tutor apologised
for her rudeness, I asked.
A blank response,
but had the seeds of doubt been sown?
Otherwise, like the paintings, nice people
warm words without engagement,
just very English.

Michelin Yum Cha Sophisticate

Me, a culinary sophisticate? Never.
But I know what I like
Simple things can taste good.
Toast, toasted cheese + tomato
Muesli + raspberries,
Not boring blueberries.
And classier formal food…
Taste buds quite good
Direction helps, Kate chose well
A good nose for quality + ambience
Then, weekend yum cha
With Tony and June
In Little Bourke St
Now Michelin One Star Chinese
Near North Point –
Tim Ho Wan.
Aircon great
Michelin new to me,
Big tyres perhaps,
Always a first for everything,
Anyway, the proof is not in the pudding
It's in the taste of the dumplings
And I am enjoying my aircon wait.
Over to you, taste buds.

Postscript
Tonic Medlar & Petal Cake
Came first
Wrong, but,
(I am an academic, after all)
'Il goût', that says *tout*
And, the *pièce de resistance*
(I always know the words!)
Hao Ji, steamed fresh shrimp dumplings
Is adjectively amazing.
So's the company
Two nice young ladies
Who gave me more to try.

Politics and Personalities

Hillary Rodham Clinton

Faces of the Donald

Bright colours
Mouth open wide, smug and blowing
Faces of the Donald
Eyes of fear…and anger
Serial groper
Big bear, small hands clapping,
Blond to red-orange visage. Warm? Hot?
Narcissistic celebrity light glowing
Brighter than grey Hillary
Pastel, with her controlled smile and
Raised eyebrows
She scripted
He maverick
Menacing, but in the journos stocks
Rotten tomatoes thrown across the Pacific
Elite condescension boosts him
His 'change' aspirations, vague,
Saving the 'people' from politicians,
Defending the 'deplorables'
Appealed to the 24%
'A ratings winner' – 'Presidential Apprentice'
People who
Wanted to believe
In a future
Even…
'Making America great again!'

Barracking for Obama

Obama came with hope in his heart
and on his lips
and HOPE on the banners
doubly an African-American
via Hawaii, Harvard and the Chicago Democrat machine
In the American era
the world cheered too,
soon a Nobel prize in his bags
Except…beyond the charm
was there a problem?
Republicans saying 'Nay' in Congress
Loud 'Noes'!
Harvard mates among his staff
Charming, brilliant, thoughtful
he and Michelle both
a beautiful couple, but…

A presidency in parts
the wit, wisdom and charm of the first family,
a young president,
increasingly, he played golf.
'He can do it!'

Worried wealthy man, Point Piper

Malcolm Says

Yes Malcolm
Not Simon says
Nor Tony declares
Or Pauline complains
Just Malcolm says
Charming persona
Colourful ties
Public smile
Harbourside pile
A reasonable man
Republican in recess
Private anger
Lawyer, banker, bully?
Cross-examining allies too
Sold his soul
To the Liberal God-squad
A Faustian bargain
'Leader' sounds good
'PM' sounds even better
Fame wanted, desperately
His $2 million donation helped
Or was it just $1.5
To buy a ticket to the Lodge
Yet the lines are spreading
A deeply furrowed brow
Tension from the chin up
Worried wealthy man, Point Piper,
Now sent back to his counting house
C'est la vie riche?

Law 'n' order populist, Peter Dutton

Laura Norder is back

A blast from the Sixties
When she saved our streets
for cars and their rights
From scruffy anti-war demonstrators
Laura Norder aka Law 'n' Order
Now she's back
And this time it's blacks
A threat to diners, says Dutton,
In Lord Rupert Moloch's
The Hun Page One
And on the *Six o'clock TV* news.
Is she now Lawn Order?
A peaceful suburban life
Free of home invaders
After our Merc keys
And mine's only a toy one, a nice light blue
Its colour matching the toy Trabant.
Dull life, bad luck,
Lying on the lounge,
Horror movie right there on my TV
Apologies Redmond and Greg,
We'll just enjoy the show,
The one created by
Laura Norder and sometimes even with
A few extra performances by
Sarah-moan-ey.

Twits, Hipsters and Digits

Self-love in the Twitsphere

Celebrities tweet
Texts of Twitter
Ripostes exchanged
On virtual golden highways
Fonts of wit
Empty of meaning
Twits doing word-selfies in 140 characters
Ordinary people forgotten
No bright lights around them
Not 'acclaimed Twitter talent'
Never 'Influencers'
Just living out their lives
On everyday streets
Deprived of virtual significance.

Digital Travels Too…Captive of the Screen

He's on the road
He's at it again
Playing with his tools
Remotes, phones, and more,
His toys
Now he has a new toy
A whole new toy box
An all-in-one toy
More than a Transformer
As he walked
It tracked him
Digitally
Offline GPS maps
Updated footy scores
Broadcasts, video clips too
Email
Pics and audio plus
Websearch
He just can't stop himself

Digital devotion
Portnoy plus!
Playing all the time
Even playing with the screen.
If he doesn't stop
Will he go blind
Or just get run over
Crossing the road?

Captive of the screen

Toxic Twits – (*Hazmat Warning!*)

The toxic twits need each other
Bilious narcissists in a few characters
Toxic Twitterati
'Influencers' so-called
Throwing Merde across the barbed wire net
A LathamM needs a FordC
'Kill all men'.
A Ford needs a Latham.
A Green Hyphen needs a Lleyonholm
'F…you too!…the feeling's mutual!'
As they grandstand
Not quite arm in arm.
'A Dolt' needs an Islamic 'Hyphen'
A Yassmin needs the Oz
Once we had thought
… And considered arguments
Now only Twits and Tweets
'All-Twitterers-are-bad!'
#Hashtagsforbrains
Or is it #Hatetags?
#Metoocleverbyhalf
But, don't forget…
Don't forget the bile.

Gone…I was completely GONE!

Gone…I was GONE
It was gone
I felt lost
Or I had lost it
Gone to a watery grave.
Was I missing my dick
Or part of my brain
Or was I now blind
And deaf
Or my hands had gone?
No 'Handy' toy to play with
Not Greek enough for worry beads
Just the e-worry box.
I had no mobile
No information
No news or weather
No train timetables
No footy scores
No music
No phone numbers
Couldn't look things up
From my golden cell,
Dr Google had deserted me
Couldn't call or text people
Worse than FOMO
This was MO totally
A capital solution
Was I dead too?

Hipsterville

Too hip for words
The pork is pulled
The avo is smashed
The dough is sour
Chai latte is so yesterday
Ristretto now
With a little something on the side
Rice, no, almond milk today
No, no, no he told the blank-faced waiter,
Ever cool, or is he just cold,
'Turmeric latte!' it will be.
Beards minceur
Florals reborn.
Narcissus lives
Hiding behind shades
No 'G'days' t'day
Not even acknowledging smiles
Welcome to hipsterville
Where 'Ken' became 'Kenso'
Good karma
But only for
Cool people like us
'Sobell'
(South of Bell)
So Green
So kind, so giving
'The working class
Can kiss my arse
I've joined the
Hipster class at last!'

Summer's Madnesses

Afternoon Sydney Summer

Afternoon Sydney summer
Sultry, not sexy
Heat and humidity
People shuffling onto the bus

Daggy, heat-daggy
Morning calm gone
Knocked out by the heat
T-shirts hanging
Some, people of size
Others, laden, tired, hot
Building workers' polos
backs marked by sweat
Fashionable girls
Make-up runny

Scruffy town,
Not international
Lawrentian still a century later,
Sweaty February
Never goes away.

All Quiet on the Summer Front

Three heat cauldrons, two passed
Shopping rushes, car chaos
Christmas Day familo-chemical stress
Three days over 35 degrees
Blasting us like heavy shelling
Air con offering only an ersatz escape
From 25 degree nights endured
I am dried out, blanched, buggered
Flattened along with the garden
Redemption possible through heavy storms
Recovery a false promise for the New Year
I must desert, run away from this battlefront,
Escape the wounds inflicted by
This unwinnable war
And find peace somewhere cold.

Everyday Life...sort of

Life's a supermarket, *c'est la vie*

La conversation du jeudi called
Despite the cold wet night
Mais, le supermarché aussi.
I left too late, the traffic was bad
And the cultures clashed.
The original natural culture – winter.
The new culture – traffic.
And roadworks clogged up
All the roads in between
Carlton was now farther from Kensington
Than when *j'ai commencé* some years ago.
My other natal culture intervened
Fused with a new culture – *le monde numérique*
Or digital apps on the phone,
The footy tipping competition
Except the mobile was slow, too slow
As I guided the trolley around *le supermarché*.
But I finally got my tips in! *
Just in time.
Mais, la conversation en français?
The watch – I still wear one –
Told me that time had moved on
And in the end I did not get there.
'Pardon Mme. C'est la vie d'aujourd'hui!'

PS * Poor tips…another story

'Can I carry Sir's books'

'Can I carry Sir's books?'
asked the Indian student
in very polite tones.
He was shorter than his subcontinental colleagues
and he looked younger as well.
I liked the Indian students even with such occasional offers.
Their spoken English was good
And they seemed natural and pleasant,
even if a few arrived on 'Delhi time'
minutes after the class started.
But there was a problem.
Some, maybe a third, maybe more, could not write English well,
certainly not academic English.
So, even more than the locals
they lived by cut and paste.
Some even winning the Mrs Trump award for plagiarism.
But they had a deal and I had a problem.
It was a three part deal and I had no hand.
They gave the government money, lots of it.
The government gave the university money, some of it.
And the uni carried their books.
It gave them passes
and in a fourth hand it gave them 'PR' –
no, not Public Relations but Permanent Residence
and I had no say in it all.
They would be good for cricket, might even like footy
but oh, I wish they hadn't carried Sir's books,
which is why Sir then carried his books away
and gave up teaching these nice young men
why Sir found other things to do.

'Retirement' matters

A heading in a PDF
From a Super fund
Yes we can 'retrie' (sic), oops, retry
(Instead of retire)
To do what we didn't achieve before
That's 'retirement' or even 'retryment'
Perhaps with a 'y'
Je suis 'SA', *'j'essaie'* (I try)
Sometimes too 'trying' I admit
While breathing I keep on trying
To create …new shticks
A lot of art, a little poetry
Even if the brand still lacks cut-through
The cost of diversity grows
I will have to try harder
With luck I'll succeed.
The joys of 'retirement'
Ongoing pleasure at last.

T'ai chi – I left my brain on Ascot Vale Road

I left my brain on Ascot Vale Road

In a quiet hall
A good teacher
Right hand on the 'dien'
Or something like that
Left hand in front of the face
Breathe in through the nose
Deeply
Out through the mouth
T'ai chi is good
Except I left my brain on Ascot Vale Road
Blocked by an ugly building going up
Detour right, then left
Oops, not that turn
Back to the main road
Missed the next left
Still breathing but…
Finally…
I made it to t'ai chi
But not quite all of me.

Hapstranging

Hanging straps
Or yellow bars too high
I don't usually catch the 8.33.

Commuting
Not quite purgatory
Not quite life.

A sardine can of bodies
Separated sometimes only by Oz
Rules about bodily space.

No reading, no 'riting
Just some mental 'rithmetic
While standing, hanging on.

Is this modern life
Hamstrung until the journey ends?

A Class Society – Cattle Class

Sheep pens
Forced feeding
Homogenised box, small
Similar taste
Doped sleeping
Waiting
No news
Body frozen
Hard to get out
Toilet queue
Ticket dollars down bowl
Screen flickering, audio crackling
Carousel congestion
Baggage wars
Jet lag kicks in.
'Have a great flight!'

A Class Society – Bourgeois Class

Turn left at the door
Bigger pens
Bone china, menus
Big napkins, spillage still
Sleeping flattish
Doped too
Delays shared
No news – 'operational reasons'
Body half frozen from inactivity
No walking down the back
Big ticket dollars down the toilet
Bigger screens, more channels
Heavy bags, sore backs
Even in what the French call
Classe affaires
Which rhymes with *le décalage horaire*
That's jet lag to you and me
Even Class J is not quite jet lag free
'Have a great flight, sir, madam'
As you may feel less well afterwards.

Issues need 'tissues'

Issues need tissues
And tissues need issues
Or…
'Ishoos' need 'tishoos'.
'It's true'
I hear you say
Angst is its own reward
Its appetite insatiable
Tears before bedtime
Lachrymose for everyone.
Once mainly girls
Now some boys too
Teardrops run down the cheeks
If you really want them to.
Of course you don't have to want them
Especially if you've run out of tissues
So sorry to hear that.
Don't worry
I'll get you some more.

Life and other catastrophes

Paper Blows Hurt

Preparing a wall
Of old rejection slips
Emails mainly
One-line rejections
After waiting four-plus months
Not the promised three
Some cut to the quick
I had heard he was a McTurd
But after the Brisbane meeting
I was flattened for three months.
Non-fiction my focus
Readable prose but only
Small print runs
And modest returns.
Me, media savvy for launches and media releases
But not quite a brand
Freelance pieces in the press
But the lance sits uneasy
Resting mostly against a wall
1984 press pay rates unchanged
Three decades later,
Article length reduced, almost halved
Rejection frequent
Not a way to earn a living.
The springs protrude from the Acca sofa
Even with its softening banknote cushions
Which I need to recover from the paper blows.

Bully in her red cell

Bullies and the Red Cell

Yes, I'd known a few
Schoolyard bullies
Thugs on the sports field
Academic managers many,
The research-free academic
Whose greatest life achievement
Was being a pre-teen mascot
For a footy club,
The militaristic woman,
More male, more Margaret
Than Thatcher herself,
The ersatz feminist
Who pursued power and her own ego
But never understood equity,
Then, finally, the research-free dean
Who built a red cell inside her palace,
Having dispensed with the peasants,
Who once occupied this space, this village agora –
The wise support staff who did good work
And lubricated the ugly machine
With humanity, calm and gentle humour.
She, who could never be a scholar or an intellectual,
Discovered her skills as an interrogator
Using her one creation,
The windowless red cell.

Formophobia

Yes, it is clear
I was not, definitely not,
Put on the earth to fill in forms.
Writing hard to read
Penmanship poor
Computer forms mock my
Proofreading skills.
Fascistic asterisks
Demand compliance.
Hidden boxes insist on ticks.
I could, I will, go on
Patience limited
Eyes for detail feeble
Numeracy not much better.
I wanna talk, I wanna dream
I want to think, I want to do –
Not fill in endless bloody forms.

'Executively developed'…almost

It sounded good, even fancy, sophisticated
'Executively developed'
A 'retreat' at a classy place
An oasis away from the urban grime of work.
Good food, some healthy, some rich
Slick facilitators, facilitating the select few.
Except…
She was a manager
Marked by a demographic scar
'Over 50' equals 'Not for promotion'.
Clever, intelligent, flexible, IT savvy
People, spreadsheet and money competent,
Innovative even.
But her cards were marked.
Real promotion was for the 'bright young things'
In tailored suits,
Glamorous post-feminists, their lustrous looks
Catching senior male managers' eyes.
She enjoyed the game, and some of the food
But she knew, deep down, that she was there as a token
An imposter.
A senior manager, Yes, but!
The escalator to the next level
She discovered, without surprise,
Was out of service when she stood before its first step.

'Swanning' by the Impatient

Suddenly, without warning,
The young neurologist swanned in
followed by his assistant
Her lanyard swinging
Her ID name also reversed.
A flotilla of cygnets followed
Med students
'Did she mind?'
'No,' she grunted politely, caught off-guard.
His manner was Oz, smiling, friendly
But casual is not engaged
Nor respectful of the 'patient'.
Then, suddenly, he – and they –
Swanned out
Our questions unasked.
Leaving no contact details…
Names, phone number of the neuros room.
She was left as a mere 'patient'
To patiently await the next sudden visit.
Except, unmoved, she remained an impatient
Wanting to be engaged with respect
R-E-S-P-E-C-T.

Grey Skies Blackening – Coronavirus 2020

Grey skies over Melbourne
light grey
a normal July but
darker clouds threatening,
lodged in our psyches
corrosive locked-down angst
rusting our optimism
across never-ending time

Mal and Genki our family

Mal and Genki Our Family

Mal and Genki were always close to us
For a third of our 34 years together
Brooding brother, hyper sister
Our feline family
A playful quartet we became.
They knew she was not well
Sitting either on her or beside her.
When she went,
Cruelly taken by MND,
Now three, we came closer together.
Mal sat on me in bed
Then wandering under the sheets
For longer than before.
Our closeness helped us all go on
Genki sat against my leg
Warming us all
Inwardly.

Life's Companion?

It was January
Sale time
Perhaps before Kate's final diagnosis
With a terminal illness.
Unlocked, cheaper than on a plan
From Dick Smith. Who?
'Life's Companion' it calls itself
A Samsung Active 4
Which might survive falls
If not sudden toilet visits.
It promised much
Emails, texts, memos,
Steps as well as calls
Inevitably, Facebook and the web
Everything except love.
Eventually, screen unresponsive
It no longer liked my fingers
I pressed and nothing happened
Or I got the bar above
'AFL Videos' not 'AFL News'
'Flight Mode' not 'Off'
Life expectancy now short?
Yet it hogged my time,
Even my mind,
Instead of conversations
And rendezvous.
More texts than calls
Emails aplenty.
Was it now my remote control?

A boy's protuberance
For playing with…compulsively.
Never leave home without it!
The best invention of the 20th century
Promised much,
But it did not offer
The fulfilment much desired
It lit up, it beeped, it rang
But it could not hug.

Significance rolls… Significant rolls

Toilet paper
Simple, long and useful
Rolls of continuity
The replenisher is ready
He ensures the future
The male as provider
Profound as well as practical
A considered approach
A symbol of significance
Of an ongoing story
Shared
A relationship
More than meets the eye
Or the derrière
Or the nose
It matters.

Naked Truths at Home and Away

Waiting for Evelyn… My Own Census Collector Lady

She leaves me cards
Tantalising ones
Every few days
Wanting my details
More than name and DOB
Am I a hot demographic perhaps?
It seems that she's watching me
Every step I take
But not yet knocking
Still I wait
For Evelyn at the door
My own census lady
Perhaps tomorrow
She will come

Moi…perdu?… The naked.truth.gov.au

Me…lost?
'Lonely, isolated?' the call centre lady asked
'No, not at all…I have you to talk to…' I replied
'Confused?'
'Well, I am an academic after all,
So what would you expect?'

But now, at last, I am a number not just a name
I exist!
Signed up to 'My Aged Care'
I now can access services
'Subsidised services' she called them,
Aka council services with the Feds' money

A compulsory 'home assessment' awaits
I think I can help them
I could present
Epidermally
… The naked truth.

Postludes

Big boss, AFL CEO Andrew Demetriou

Footy's changed

Once upon a time
after school
we played kick to kick
and scratch matches
on the school gravel
however many a side
jumpers and bags for goalposts
imagined taking screamers
disputed goals – 'it was touched'.
I nearly cried after losing.
No marbles today either.

We went to the footy
stood on cans
tried to see.
A kick after the game
was the highlight!

Now, it's different.
Stadiums not grounds
gotta book seats
packaged entertainment
dumb announcers
loud PA
can't hear footy on my radio.

Game's now changed.
'Whatever it takes!'
Drugs, gyms, stats.
On the field it's
mostly clogged
some keepings off
tackles first, rugby now
high marks nowhere.
Scripted play, not footy.

After the match too
players spouting media clichés.
'We kept to our structures…
I played my role'
mumbled the star.

After-school footy was so much better.
We played the game at a higher level.

Definitely Not a Poet – Clayton's Postlude… Retrospective Overture

    Yes, you can write, mate
    And, some of the time,
Write very well
    'But, maaate,' he said
    In his Bob Hawke gravelly Labor voice,
    Giving a tap on the shoulder,
'You ain't no poet
    Why don't you know it?'
    Well, Pete, you can defend your
Vegie patch
    Carefully cultivated with
Horse poo
    Or is it high-quality
Cow dung
    Anyway, maate, you can have
Your genre
    But you better duck
    While I throw some more
Merde at you.

Definitely Not a Poet, Maate!

'You're not a poet'
He declared
Pithily, I mean bluntly,
Not enough nature
No seasons of significance
No falling autumn leaves
Or fading sunsets
Metaphors abundant.
You are lacking
In poetic lyricism
Poesy's images
Cultured references
Words worth having,
Emotions
Recollected
In tranquillity,
Not to mention
Meaningful pauses,
Subtle silences,
Moral reflections,
Moments of doubt,
A grave tone and
A poetic timbre.
I discern a veritable absence
Of ersatz meaningfulness.
Quite a lot really.
Lines too long,
Tone too conversational,
Words too everyday,
'Why not try some other form!' declared Pete, the 'Poet Proper'.

www.ingramcontent.com/pod-product-compliance
Lightning Source LLC
Chambersburg PA
CBHW062148100526
44589CB00014B/1740